Life Cycle of a

Bean

Angela Royston

Heinemann Library
Chicago, Illinois

Designed by Celia Floyd
Illustrations by Alan Fraser
Printed and bound in Hong Kong/China

02 01 00
10 9 8 7 6 5 4

Library of Congress Cataloging-in-Publication Data
Royston, Angela.
    Life cycle of a bean / by Angela Royston.
        p.   cm.
    Includes index.
    Summary: An introduction to the life cycle of a bean from the time
it is first planted until, four months later, it has grown as tall
as an adult person.
    ISBN 1-57572-612-2 (lib. bdg.)
    I. Fava bean--Life cycles--Juvenile literature.   [1. Beans.]
I. Title.
SB351.F3R69 1998
583'.74--dc21   97-39693
                                                        CIP
                                                        AC

Acknowledgements
The Publisher would like to thank the following for permission to reproduce
photographs:
A–Z Botanical Collection/Moira C Smith p10; Bruce Coleman/Adrian Davies p23;
Chris Honeywell pp17, 18; Harry Smith Collection pp6, 14, 20, 21, 22, 26/27;
Heather Angel p13; OSF/G A Maclean p19; OSF/G I Bernard pp7, 8, 9; OSF/J A L
Cooke p12; The Garden Picture Library/David Askham p25; The Garden Picture
Library/Mayer Le Scanff p5; The Garden Picture/Michael Howes pp11, 24;
Roger Scruton p4; Trevor Clifford p15.

Cover photograph: Trevor Clifford

Some words are shown in bold, **like this**. You can find out what they
mean by looking in the glossary.

Contents

What are Beans?

Beans are **seeds** that grow in **pods**. We eat many kinds of beans including kidney beans, black-eyed peas, and fava beans.

1 day   1 week   2 weeks   6 weeks

These are fava beans. This book
shows what happens to a fava
bean when it is planted.

12 weeks

14 weeks

20 weeks

6

The bean **seed** is planted in the **soil** with other bean seeds. The soil is watered and the beans begin to grow.

1 day

1 week

2 weeks

6 weeks

root

First a **root** grows. It pushes
through the bean seed and grows
down into the soil. It grows longer
and longer.

12 weeks   14 weeks   20 weeks

Sprouting

Now the bean is sprouting. A **shoot** starts to grow. The bent **stem** pushes up through the **soil**. At the end of the stem are tiny leaves.

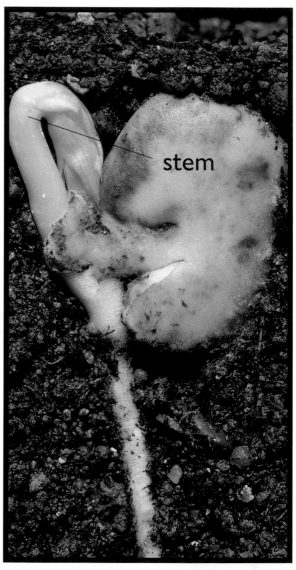

stem

 I day I week 2 weeks 6 weeks

The shoot has pushed up through the soil. The stem straightens and the leaves begin to open. More **roots** are growing.

roots

12 weeks

14 weeks

20 weeks

Growing
3 to10 weeks

The leaves open out and turn dark green in the light. The leaves use sunlight, air, and water to make food for the plant to grow.

| 1 day | 1 week | 2 weeks | 6 weeks |

Water from the **soil** passes into the **roots** and goes through the **stem** up to the leaves. The plant grows quickly. Flower buds begin to form.

12 weeks   14 weeks   20 weeks

12

A blackfly lays her eggs under some of the leaves. These blackflies have **hatched** from their eggs and are eating the leaves.

| 1 day | 1 week | 2 weeks | 6 weeks |

If the plant's leaves become
too damaged, the plant will die.
Ladybugs eat the blackflies and
help to save the plant.

12 weeks

14 weeks

20 weeks

Flowering 12 weeks

Thick bunches of flowers open
at the bottom of the leaves. The
petals are black and white.

 1 day

 1 week

 2 weeks

 6 weeks

In the center of each flower are tiny grains of **pollen** and a sweet juice called nectar. Insects come to drink the nectar.

15

12 weeks

The bee crawls right into the flower. As it sips the nectar, grains of **pollen** collect on its hairy legs.

1 day   1 week   2 weeks   6 weeks

At the same time, some of the pollen from another flower rubs off inside this one. This is called pollination.

12 weeks   14 weeks 20 weeks

Bean Pods   12 to 14 weeks

When a grain of **pollen** from one flower joins a **seed** inside another flower, it becomes a new bean seed. The flower dies and the beans swell.

1 day   1 week   2 weeks   6 weeks

pods

The beans are protected inside a tough, thick **pod**. As the beans grow, the pod grows longer and heavier.

12 weeks

14 weeks

20 weeks

These bean plants are growing many **pods.**

20

1 day   1 week   2 weeks   6 weeks

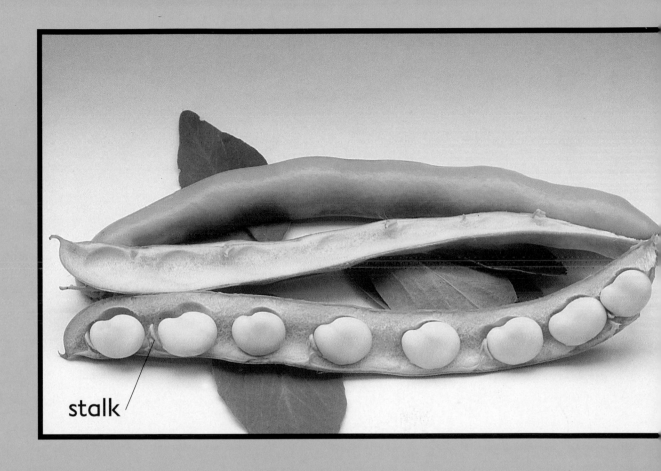

stalk

The inside of the pod is soft and damp. Each bean is joined to the pod by a short stalk. The stalk brings food and water to the bean.

Fully Grown

20 weeks

When the beans are fully grown, the **pod** begins to turn black. The plant has done its job and the leaves begin to die.

Some of the pods fall to the ground and split open. Field mice like to eat the beans. Some of the beans will replant themselves.

12 weeks 14 weeks 20 weeks

Picking Beans 20 to 24 weeks

24

Most beans are picked before they are fully grown. They are more juicy to eat then.

1 day   1 week   2 weeks   6 weeks

Not all of the beans are eaten.
As they dry, they turn hard and
brown. These new **seeds** will be
planted to grow new beans.

12 weeks   14 weeks   20 weeks

A Field of Beans

Farmers plant beans in huge fields like this one. The **pods** are picked and most are sent to factories to be frozen or put into cans.

The old plants will be cut up and
covered with **soil**. As the plants
rot, they will slowly break up and
become part of the soil.

Life Cycle

Seeds

1

Roots

2

Sprouting

3

Growing

4

Flowering

5

Bean Pods

6

Picking Beans

7

Fact File

In just four months a fava bean grows from a **seed** to a plant as tall as an adult person.

One fava bean plant can produce over 300 beans.

In Ancient Greece and Rome, rich people would not eat fava beans because they thought they would damage their sight.

Glossary

hatch   to be born out of an egg

pod   a tough, thick shell that
  beans grow in

pollen   fine yellow dust made in
  the center of a flower

root   part of a plant under the
  ground which takes in water and
  food from the soil

seed   the part of a plant which
  can grow into a new plant

shoot   the first stem and leaves
  of a new plant

soil   the ground the plant grows in

stem   the stalk that supports the
  leaves, flowers, and fruit of a plant

More Books to Read

Goldish, Meish. *How Plants Get Food*. Chatham, NJ: Raintree Steck-Vaughn. 1989.

Kuchalla, Susan. *All About Seeds*. Mahway, NJ: Troll Communications L.L.C. 1982.

Rowe, Julia & Perham, Molly. *Watch it Grow!* Danbury, CT: Children's Press. 1994.

Index